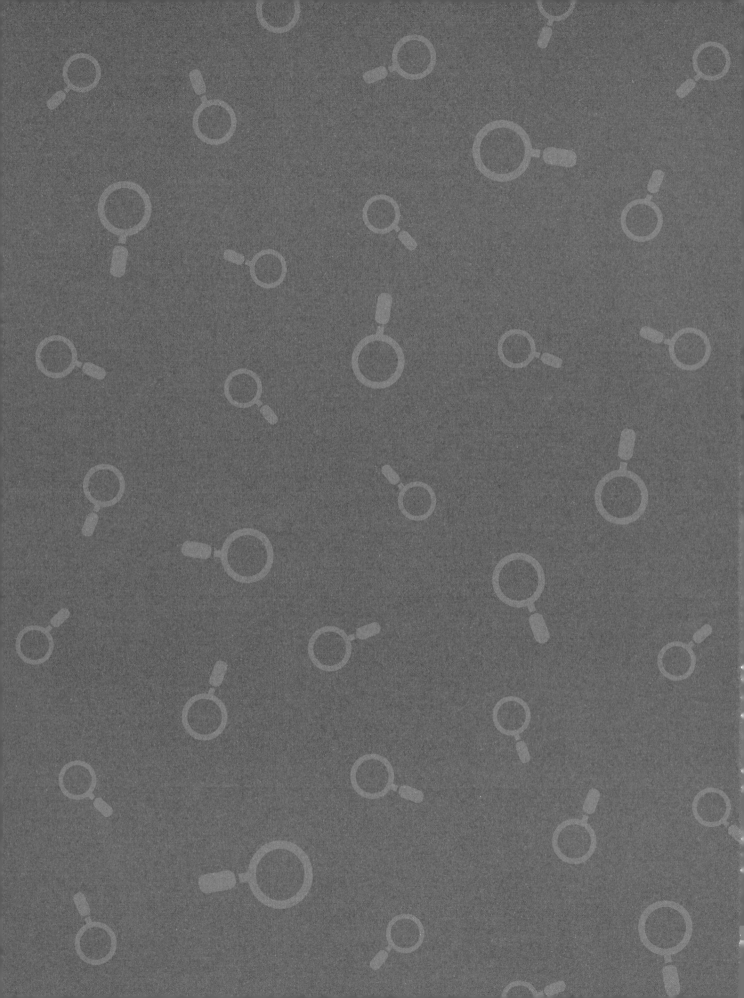

DISCOVER AND DO!

ANCIENT EGYPTIANS
GET HANDS-ON WITH HISTORY

Written by Jane Lacey

W
FRANKLIN WATTS
LONDON • SYDNEY

Franklin Watts
First published in Great Britain in 2021
by The Watts Publishing Group
Copyright © The Watts Publishing Group, 2021

Produced for Franklin Watts by
White-Thomson Publishing Ltd
www.wtpub.co.uk

HB ISBN: 978 1 4451 7726 7
PB ISBN: 978 1 4451 7754 0

Editor: Izzi Howell
Designer: Clare Nicholas
Series designer: Rocket Design (East Anglia) Ltd

Picture credits:
t=top b=bottom m=middle l=left r=right

Getty: ikryannikovgmailcom 6l and 29b, PeterHermesFurian
8t, SSPL 23t, Abrill_ 24t; The Metropolitan Museum of Art:
Rogers Fund, 1908 15t, Rogers Fund and Edward S. Harkness
Gift, 1920 16b, Rogers Fund, 1934 21t; Shutterstock: cover
and title page Elegant Solution, klyaksun 4, 5tr, 22b and
31t, GoodStudio 5tl and 14b, OlgaChernyak 5b and 18,
vectorpouch 6r, Olga Kuevda 7t, 8b and 31b, Cortyn 10t
and 32, tan_tan 10b, matrioshka 11, Federico Rostagno 12t,
HappyPictures 12b, Dario Lo Presti 16t and 30t, Lars Poyansky
17t and 29t, Liudmila Klymenko 20t, PremiumStock 20bl and
28, Ashwin 20br, Eroshka 22t, Pavel Kukol 24b, Eugene Li
25t, Love Lego 26l, Colin Hayes 26r and 31c; Walters Art
Museum: Acquired by Henry Walters, 1909 14t and 30b.

All design elements from Shutterstock.
Craft models from a previous series made by
Anna-Marie D'Cruz/photos by Steve Shott.

Every attempt has been made to clear copyright.
Should there be any inadvertent omission, please
apply to the publisher for rectification.

Printed in China

Franklin Watts
An imprint of
Hachette Children's Group
Part of The Watts Publishing Group
Carmelite House
50 Victoria Embankment
London EC4Y 0DZ

An Hachette UK Company
www.hachettechildrens.co.uk

ANCIENT EGYPTIANS
GET HANDS-ON WITH HISTORY

W

FRANKLIN WATTS

LONDON • SYDNEY

CONTENTS

Words that appear in **bold** can be found in the glossary on pages 28–29.

THE EGYPTIANS

The Ancient Egyptians lived near the banks of the River Nile in Egypt. There was plenty of water and the soil was good for farming. Their **civilisation** started in 3,100 BCE and ended in 30 BCE when Egypt became part of the Roman Empire.

Egyptian civilisation

The Egyptians were ruled by a king called a **pharaoh**. They were clever **engineers** who built cities with magnificent palaces, temples and **tombs**. The remains of pots, weapons, tools and jewellery found show that they were also skilled craftsmen.

This is the funeral mask of the Pharaoh Tutankhamun.

The Egyptians built some buildings that were meant to last forever. They were made of stone. Some still survive today.

Trade

Egypt was a wealthy country. Egyptian traders sold their **goods** to Africa, the Mediterranean and far-away India. They brought back exotic animals, ivory, timber, silk and perfume.

Egyptian traders travelled by ship to trade goods.

THE RIVER NILE

The River Nile is the longest river in the world. It runs through the North African desert and out into the Mediterranean Sea.

Floods

Snow melting in the mountains in the south floods the Nile every year in June. The floodwater leaves behind **silt**, which makes the soil good for farming.

The Nile is surrounded by hot, dry desert where it hardly ever rains.

Farming

The Ancient Egyptians settled along the banks of the River Nile and farmers planted crops in the rich soil. Their year was divided into three seasons called flood, crop sowing and harvesting. As there was little rain, farmers cut **irrigation canals** to carry water from the river to the fields and villages.

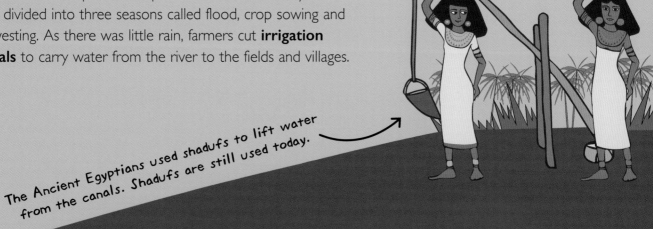

The Ancient Egyptians used shadufs to lift water from the canals. Shadufs are still used today.

MAKE A SHADUF

You will need:
- **four sticks of dowel**
  (3x 20 cm and 1x 30 cm)
- **string or twine**
- **Plasticine**
- **foil**

1 Tie together the three 20-cm dowels, 3 cm from one end. Spread them into a triangular frame. Press the ends into a Plasticine base.

2 Loosely tie the 30-cm dowel to the top of the frame, about 4 cm from one end.

3 Add a lump of Plasticine to make a counterweight to the short end.

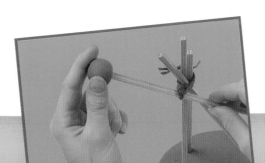

4 Shape a bucket from foil. Hang it from the other end of the lever with a piece of long string.

5 Try it out. Pull the string down to fill the bucket with water. Push down on the weight to lift the bucket of water.

EGYPTIAN LIFE

Keeping cool and growing enough food to eat was an important part of Egyptian daily life.

Houses

Egyptian houses were built to keep out the heat. The walls were painted white to reflect the sun. Windows were small and high and vents in the roofs and walls trapped the cool North winds.

Houses were made from mud bricks strengthened with straw and baked hard in the sun. You can still find houses in Egypt made like this.

Nobles to slaves

Wealthy **nobles** served in the Pharaoh's court. Educated **scribes** kept important records, and priests ran the temples. There were many traders and skilled craftsmen but most people were peasants who belonged to the landowners. There were also **slaves**.

Craftsmen made many different objects by hand, such as sculptures, jewellery and tools.

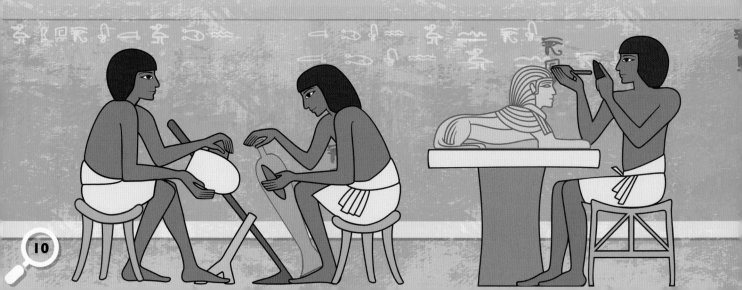

Food

Rich soil alongside the Nile meant the Egyptians could grow lots of food for festivals and feasts. Bread and cakes were made from wheat and barley. Figs, dates and grapes were either eaten fresh, or dried and stored, or made into wine. They caught fish from the river.

Egyptian paintings show people harvesting fruit and catching fish.

ACTIVITY

MAKE A FAN

You will need:
- **card (white, gold, purple and green)**
- **strong brown card**
- **scissors**

1 Cut out about 30 feather shapes (below) from white card, about 16 cm long.

3 Copy and cut out the handle (left) from strong brown card. Make it 20 cm long.

Handle

Feathers

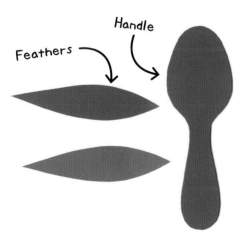

4 Stick the white feathers onto the back of the handle, adding the coloured feathers to make a pattern. Use your fan to keep cool.

2 Cut out feathers in gold, purple and green card, three in each colour.

CLOTHES

Egyptian clothes were made from **linen**. They were light and loose for keeping cool in the heat. Men's **kilts** and women's dresses were often pressed into pleats. Farmers wore **loin cloths** to work in the fields while children went naked in the heat.

Linen

Linen was made from the fibres of the flax plant. First the flax heads were removed with a type of comb. Then the stems were soaked, beaten and combed until they were ready for spinning into thread.

Nets

Nets helped to protect linen clothes from wearing out too quickly. Soldiers wore leather nets over their kilts and women servants wore beaded nets over their dresses.

Clothes were usually white, the natural colour of the linen cloth, like the Egyptians are wearing in this wall painting.

All of the beaded nets were made by hand.

MAKE EGYPTIAN SANDALS

The Egyptians wore sandals that were made from papyrus – a kind of reed that grows on the banks of the Nile.

Ask an adult to help you with this activity.

You will need:
- **thick carboard**
- **scissors**
- **hole punch**
- **brown ribbon**

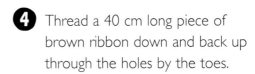

1 Draw round your feet on a piece of thick cardboard. Mark two spots between your big toe and second toe. Mark a spot on either side of the heel.

2 Ask an adult to help cut out the thick cardboard soles and punch holes on the marked spots.

3 Tie two 10 cm long pieces of brown ribbon in the holes by the heel, one in each.

4 Thread a 40 cm long piece of brown ribbon down and back up through the holes by the toes.

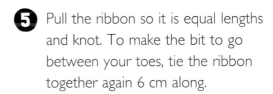

5 Pull the ribbon so it is equal lengths and knot. To make the bit to go between your toes, tie the ribbon together again 6 cm along.

6 Tie the ends of the ribbons in bows around your foot. Finish the sandal for your other foot and try them on.

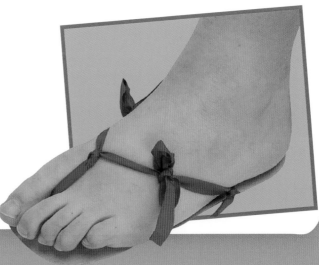

HAIR AND MAKE-UP

Most Egyptians wore some jewellery. Ordinary people wore copper rings and **amulets** to keep away evil spirits. Jewellery for wealthy Egyptians was made of gold from Egypt's own gold mines. Collars, rings, ear studs, bracelets and **anklets** were set with colourful semi-precious stones.

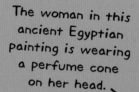

The woman in this ancient Egyptian painting is wearing a perfume cone on her head.

Wigs and wax

Egyptians wore long, black, plaited wigs. A cone of scented wax worn on top of the head melted in the heat and trickled down the wearer's wig, making them smell nice.

Both men and women outlined their eyes with black make-up.

Make-up

The Egyptians used mirrors, combs, tweezers and make-up to achieve the style of the time. Coloured minerals were ground into powder and mixed with wax to make black eye paint and red rouge for lips and cheeks.

MAKE A DECORATED COLLAR

Decorated collars added richness and colour to the plain linen clothes.

You will need:

- **large piece of card**
- **hole punch**
- **scissors**
- **paint, various colours**
- **drinking straws, various colours**
- **sequins**
- **ribbon**

1 Copy the shape of the collar. Make it as wide as your shoulders. Punch holes in the top as shown.

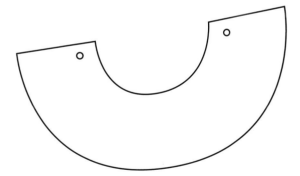

2 Cut coloured straws into 2-cm lengths. Decorate the collar with alternate stripes of paint, rows of coloured straws and sequins.

Craftsmen moulded, beat and carved metal into jewellery like this collar.

3 Thread with ribbon and wear your Egyptian collar.

DAILY LIFE

The Ancient Egyptians wrote in **hieroglyphs**.
Some of the words looked like pictures.
For hundreds of years, historians
could not understand the hieroglyphs.

The Rosetta Stone

In 1799, the Rosetta stone was found. The same words
were written in three different languages: Greek,
Demotic and hieroglyphs. This meant that scholars
could now translate hieroglyphs for the first time.

The Rosetta stone
unlocked the ancient
secrets of the
hieroglyphs.

Scribes

Very few people could read and write hieroglyphs. There were
about 700 signs to learn. Scribes started their training as young boys
and took many years to learn to read and write hieroglyphs.

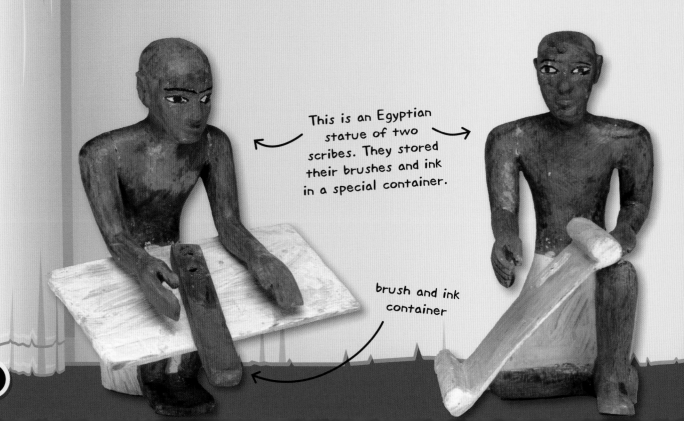

This is an Egyptian
statue of two
scribes. They stored
their brushes and ink
in a special container.

brush and ink
container

Papyrus

Papyrus was a kind of paper made of pith from the stem of the papyrus reed. Strips of pith were laid criss-cross on a frame and flattened under heavy weights to make sheets.

Scribes wrote hieroglyphs on pieces of papyrus.

ACTIVITY

WRITE YOUR NAME IN HIEROGLYPHS

Hieroglyphs were either a whole word or a single letter. The name of a pharaoh was written on an oval **cartouche**.

2 Design a cartouche around it, colouring it with vivid colours as if you were the king!

You will need:
- **paper**
- **pens or pencils, various colours**

1 Write your name in hieroglyphs, using the key below.

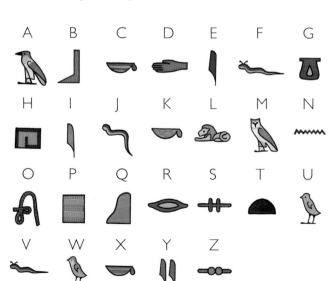

GODS AND GODDESSES

The Ancient Egyptians worshipped many hundreds of gods and goddesses. They believed in life after death and tried to make sure they would make it safely to the spirit world. Pharaohs went to a special place when they died called 'the land of the gods'.

The gods

Egyptians believed that the gods controlled human beings and all of nature.

Re was the sun god and creator of men.

Thoth, the moon god of wisdom, had a curved beak of a sacred ibis.

Isis was the goddess of women and children.

Horus, protector of Pharaohs, had a falcon's head.

Anubis was the jackal-headed god of death, rebirth and mummification.

Khnum was the ram-headed god of the Nile.

MAKE A HEAD OF THE GODDESS BASTET

Re's daughter, a cat called Bastet, was the goddess of the harvest.

You will need:
- **newspaper**
- **cardboard tube**
- **masking tape**
- **PVA glue**
- **water**
- **paint (green, yellow and gold)**

1 Scrunch up some newspaper to make a fist-sized ball. Put it on top of a cardboard tube and fix it to the tube with masking tape.

2 Mix a little PVA glue with water in a bowl. Tear up small pieces of newspaper and put them in the bowl to soak.

3 Shape two thick triangles from glue-soaked newspaper for ears and a strip for the nose. Fix with papier mâché strips.

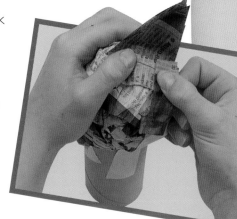

4 Cover the head with a layer of papier mâché. Leave to dry thoroughly.

5 Paint dark green all over and make the eyes yellow. Use gold paint to mark on earrings and a jewel on the forehead.

THE PHARAOH

The Pharaoh was the king of Egypt. The Egyptians believed that the Pharaoh was a god and that his wife was a goddess. A boy born to be the Pharaoh learnt to hunt, to fight and to lead his army in battle. The Pharaoh was also a high priest in the temple.

Ramses the Great ordered the building of the Abu Simbel temple. It has large statues of Ramses outside.

Famous Pharaohs

Ramses the Great built many great buildings and monuments. The ruins of these can still be seen today. Similarly, jewellery, clothes and weapons from the tomb of the Pharaoh Tutankhamun tell us a great deal about Ancient Egypt.

War

The Pharaoh went to war to protect his land against hostile armies or to take over another country. He rode in a horse-drawn chariot and carried a bow and arrow.

Tutankhamun rode into battle in a chariot.

A Pharaoh had coloured crowns for different occasions. He wore different-coloured crowns in different parts of Egypt, and another colour in times of war.

This is a statue of King Seti II. His crown was originally painted blue. ➜

MAKE A PHARAOH'S BLUE CROWN

You will need:
- **card (blue and gold)**
- **scissors**
- **black marker pen**
- **gold paint, optional**

❷ Decorate it with gold spots, a coiled cobra and a golden sun disk.

❸ Make a band of gold card to go around your head. Attach the blue crown and wear it.

❶ Copy and cut out the shape of the crown on blue card. Make it about the width of your head.

TEMPLE LIFE

Egyptian temples were huge. They were built of stone because they were meant to last forever. Priests performed temple rituals, such as offering gifts to the gods. Only high priests and the Pharaoh went into the inner temple. Ordinary people were allowed into the temple courtyard for festivals.

Around the temple

The temple gate was called a pylon. Statues of the Pharaoh stood at the gate. Tall, thin **obelisks** carved with messages to the gods marked the point where the first rays of the sun fell. **Sphinxes** guarded the avenue in front of the temple.

High priests wore leopard skins.

Temple walls were painted and carved with *stories of gods and Pharaohs.*

sphinxes

The hour-watcher priest

The hour-watcher priest was in charge of making sure the temple rituals were carried out on time. By day, he kept time by the sun. At night, he used a water clock. Water dripped slowly from a hole in the bottom of a special container. It took an hour for the water level to drop from one mark to the next.

A water clock from Ancient Egypt.

ACTIVITY

MAKING A WATER CLOCK

Ask an adult to help you with this activity.

You will need:
- **large paper cup**
- **safety pin**
- **black paper**
- **white paint pen (or other pen that will write on black paper)**
- **water**
- **tall drinking glass**
- **waterproof pen**
- **clock or watch**

1 Make a very small hole in the base of a large paper cup with a safety pin (ask an adult to help).

2 Tape some black paper around the cup. Decorate it with Egyptian figures and hieroglyphs.

3 Fill the cup with water and suspend it in a tall glass.

4 How long does it take to empty? Mark the level of the water every 5 minutes with a waterproof pen on the inside of the cup.

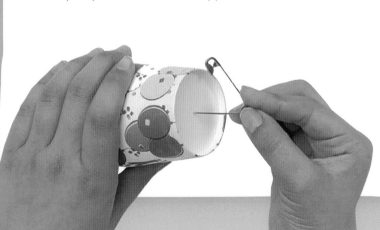

THE PYRAMIDS

Egypt's great **pyramids** were tombs for some of the Pharaohs and their families. Each Pharaoh's body was laid in a chamber deep inside the pyramid where it was protected from the heat, and from robbers and animals. The burial chamber was filled with things the Pharaoh would need in the **afterlife**.

The pyramid shape

The shape of the pyramid was built to look like the mound that rose from water at the beginning of time, as told in Egyptian **myths**. The sun god Re stood on the mound's peak and called up all the other gods and goddesses.

The four sides of the pyramids faced north, south, east and west.

The insides of burial chambers were decorated with pictures and writing.

The great pyramid

The great pyramid at Giza is about 4,500 years old. It was the tomb of King Khufu. The workers building the pyramid had no pulleys, only levers and rollers to move two million blocks of stone. It took about 20 years to build one huge pyramid.

The sides of the pyramids look smooth but they are actually made out of many large stone blocks.

ACTIVITY

MAKE A PYRAMID

You will need:
- **yellow card**
- **scissors**
- **glue or tape**
- **paints or pens for decorating**

1 Copy the pattern of a four-sided pyramid onto yellow card and cut out. Include a flap on one edge.

3 Paint details on the pyramid. You could add a burial chamber in a small box inside.

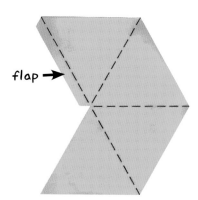

flap →

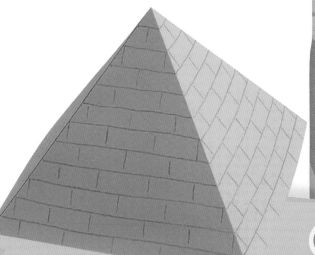

2 Fold along the dotted lines and stick the flap to form a pyramid shape.

THE AFTERLIFE

The Ancient Egyptians believed in life after death. They thought they needed their body in the afterlife so they took great care to **preserve** dead bodies. This was done by a process called mummification.

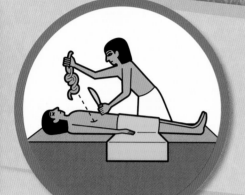

Mummification

Mummification was carried out by **embalmers**. The heart was left in the body.

1 The lungs, stomach, intestines and liver were removed, dried and put in canopic jars.

2 The brain was pulled out through the nose with a hook.

3 The body was dried, the face was decorated with make-up and a wig was put on.

4 Then the body was rubbed with scented oil, covered in resin and wrapped in linen.

Canopic jars often had decorated lids in the shape of gods and other important figures.

MAKE CANOPIC JARS

You will need:

- four small glass jars
- paper
- pens or paints for decorating
- tape
- scissors
- orange peel
- small pink balloon
- dried noodle nest
- brown paint
- tea bag or coffee filter
- cling film

1 Copy the pictures of the four sons of Horus onto strips of paper to decorate the four glass jars.

2 To make the lungs, cut out shapes of lungs in orange peel and dry them out. For the stomach, blow up a small pink balloon then let out the air.

3 Make the intestines by painting dried noodles brown and dark red. The liver is a dried-out used tea bag or coffee filter wrapped in cling film. Put each in its right jar.

Hapi – baboon-headed god who protected the lungs.

Duamutef – jackal-headed god who protected the stomach.

Qebehsenuef – falcon-headed god who protected the intestines.

Imsety – human-headed god who protected the liver.

Glossary

afterlife

The afterlife is a life after death. The Egyptians believed they lived on in another place after they died.

amulet

An amulet is a charm worn as protection against evil spirits.

anklet

An anklet is jewellery worn around the ankle.

canopic jar

A canopic jar is a jar used in Ancient Egypt to hold organs of the body.

civilisation

A civilisation is an organised society, usually based around a city.

embalmer

An embalmer is someone who treats a dead body to stop it decaying.

engineer

An engineer is someone who designs and builds machines and buildings.

goods

Goods are things that are bought and sold such as food, cloth and jewels.

hieroglyph

A hieroglyph is a symbol or picture used for writing. The Ancient Egyptians wrote in hieroglyphics.

irrigation canal

An irrigation canal is a ditch carrying water from a lake or river to fields where crops grow.

kilt

A kilt is a pleated, knee-length skirt.

linen

Linen is cloth woven from threads spun from the flax plant.

loin cloth

A loin cloth is a cloth tied round the hips and between the legs.

mummification

Mummification is a way of keeping a dead body from decaying by treating it with oils and wrapping it in cloth.

myth

A myth is an old story about gods and heroes in ancient times.

noble

A noble is someone with wealth and power in a royal court or government.

obelisk

An obelisk is a monument in the shape of a flat-sided pillar with a pointed top like a pyramid.

pharaoh

A pharaoh was a king of Ancient Egypt.

preserve

To preserve is to keep something from decaying or rotting.

pyramid

A pyramid is a shape with a square base and triangular walls. Some Egyptian royalty were buried in giant pyramids.

resin

Resin is a sticky tree sap that was used by embalmers in mummification.

scribe

A scribe is someone who writes documents by hand. Ancient Egyptian scribes wrote in hieroglyphics.

silt

Silt is tiny pieces of mud or clay carried along by rivers. Silt helps to make soil rich for farming.

sphinx

A sphinx is a creature with a lion's body and the head of a man, a ram or a bird.

tomb

A tomb is a grave, or a cave or a building that contains a grave.

Quiz

① Which river did the Ancient Egyptians live near?

a) River Ganges
b) River Congo
c) River Thames
d) River Nile

② What did scribes do?

a) work on farms
b) read and write hieroglyphs
c) work in a temple
d) take care of the pharaoh

③ From which material were Egyptian clothes made?

a) linen
b) wool
c) papyrus
d) silk

④ What did Egyptian wigs look like?

a) short, grey plaits
b) hair of many different colours
c) short blond curly hair
d) long, black plaits

⑤ Which object helped historians understand hieroglyphs?

a) the Rosetta stone
b) papyrus scrolls
c) a shaduf
d) the great pyramid

⑥ Who was the Egyptian sun god?

a) Anubis
b) Thoth
c) Re
d) Isis

⑦ Which animal did the god Horus have the head of?

a) leopard
b) falcon
c) cat
d) crocodile

⑧ Which weapon did the pharaoh use?

a) sword
b) cannon
c) spear
d) bow and arrow

9 **Who was allowed into the inner temple?**

a) high priests and the pharaoh
b) no one
c) everyone
d) only the pharaoh

10 **Which body part was left inside a mummy?**

a) brain
b) stomach
c) heart
d) lungs

ANSWERS 1d, 2b, 3a, 4d, 5a, 6c, 7b, 8d, 9a, 10c

FURTHER INFORMATION

BOOKS

Ancient Egyptians (History in Infographics) by Jon Richards and Jonathan Vipond, Wayland

Explore! Ancient Egyptians by Jane Bingham, Wayland

The Genius of: the Ancient Egyptians by Sonya Newland, Franklin Watts

Truth or Busted: The Fact or Fiction Behind the Egyptians by Kay Barnham, Wayland

WEBSITES

Discover 10 fun facts about the Ancient Egyptians www.natgeokids.com/uk/discover/history/egypt/ten-facts-about-ancient-egypt/

Learn more about what life was like in Ancient Egypt www.bbc.co.uk/bitesize/topics/zg87xnb/articles/zr4s8xs/

Find out more about the pyramids www.dkfindout.com/uk/history/ancient-egypt/pyramids/

Read more about hieroglyphs www.childrensuniversity.manchester.ac.uk/learning-activities/history/ancient-egypt/writing-in-hieroglyphs/

Index

Titles in the DISCOVER AND DO! HISTORY series

- Invasion
- Warriors
- Settlers
- Village life
- Clothes
- Storytellers
- Death and burial
- Kings and kingdoms
- Gods and goddesses
- Religion
- Runes and writing

- The Egyptians
- The River Nile
- Egyptian life
- Clothes
- Hair and make-up
- Writing
- Gods and goddesses
- The Pharaoh
- Temple life
- The pyramids
- The afterlife

- The Greeks
- City states
- Daily life
- Childhood
- Clothes
- Religion and myths
- Olympic games
- Writing
- Theatre
- Learning
- Famous Greeks

- The Romans
- Roman emperors
- The army
- Life in Roman times
- Houses
- Childhood
- Letters and numbers
- Entertainment
- Roman baths
- Roman towns
- Gods and myths

- The Tudors
- Henry VIII
- Life at court
- Tudor homes
- Tudor London
- Street life
- Elizabeth I
- Exploration
- Tudor childhood
- Food
- Theatre

- The Vikings
- Sea journeys
- Warriors
- Viking raids
- Viking houses
- Daily life
- Viking crafts
- Pastimes
- Life and death
- Gods and legends
- Famous Vikings

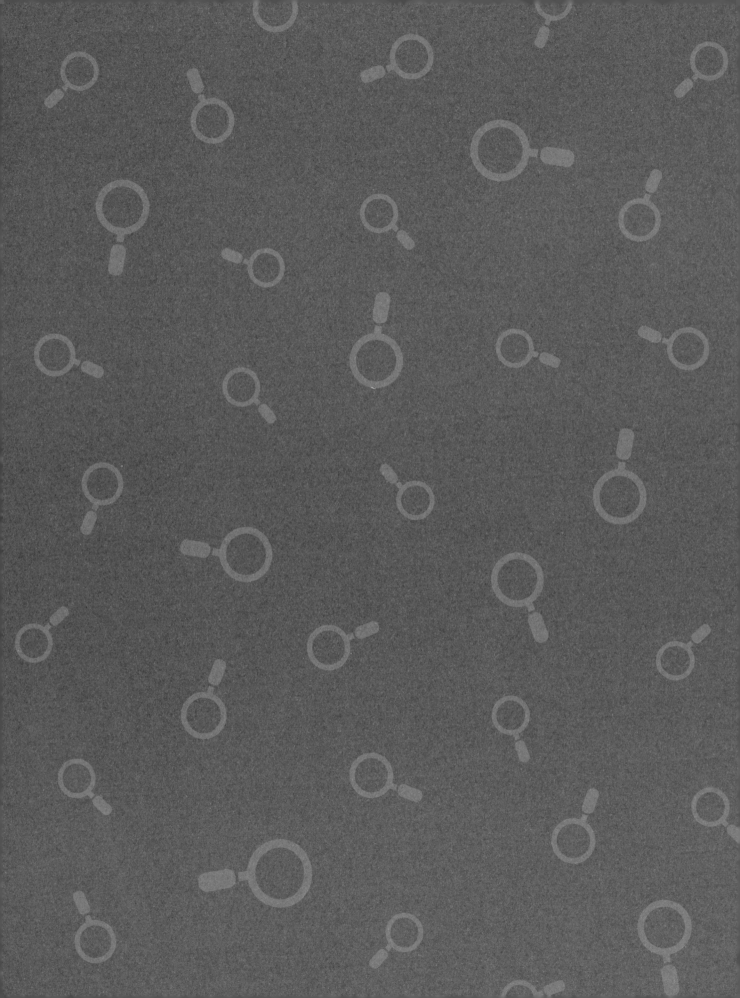